Prayers for Those with Dementia

Chosen and illustrated
by Chris Coe

**kevin
mayhew**

These moving prayers and reflections are
for the ever-increasing number of people
who live with the challenge of dementia,
whether having been diagnosed themselves
or caring for a loved one.

They do not shrink from the feelings of
helplessness and confusion that accompany
dementia but they do offer insight
and understanding.

As you read them remember that the
entire Church of God is praying with you,
holding you in its hands, just as our Saviour,
Jesus, holds you in his arms.

Loving God,
when life is hard and days are dark,
enfold me in your arms and surround me
with your loving care,
holding me close for all eternity.

Nick Fawcett

The Lord is my light and my salvation

Psalm 27:1

God will be our guide for ever

Psalm 48:14

When we can
no longer walk,
God carries us.
When we get ourselves lost,
the Good Shepherd is out
searching for us
and hears our bleating.
And when he finds us
he lifts us on his shoulders
and brings us safely home.

Susan Sayers

Hold My Hand

Hold my hand, Lord.
Walk me through the loneliness
and the valley of my sorrow.
Hold on to me when I'm afraid
to think about tomorrow.
Let me lean on you, Lord,
when I'm too weary to go on.
Hold my hand, Lord,
through the night
until I see the light of dawn.

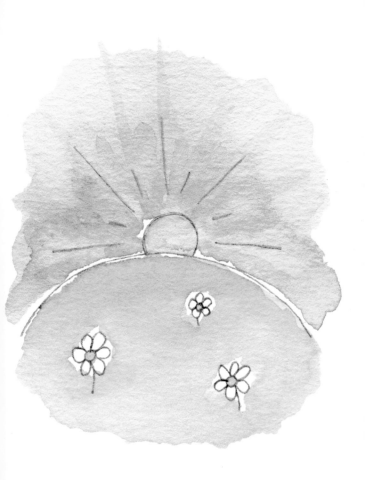

The Lord is my helper, I will not be afraid

Hebrews 13:6

May mercy, peace and love be yours in abundance

Jude, verse 2

Gracious God,
when the world seems bleak
and all seems lost,
remind me that through the agony
and desolation of the cross
you were supremely at work
bringing light out of the darkness,
hope out of despair, good out of evil
and life out of death.
So help me to look at the future with faith
and to face the present at peace.

Nick Fawcett

If everything feels tightly
knotted and tangled,
stop tugging at it
and allow God
to work it out.

Susan Sayers

The God of peace will be with you

Philippians 4:9

Look to the Lord and his strength;
seek his face always

Psalm 105:4

Christ, you invite us to pray
with great faith and confidence
for all who suffer any disability or illness.
You wish to bestow your gift of peace on all.

Disability, brokenness, memory loss,
confusion, communication difficulties,
challenging behaviours, disorientation, fragility:
these do not exclude anyone
from the unconditional promises of God.
He reminds us, 'Do not fear, only believe.'

Siobhán O'Keeffe

Loving God,
in the unpredictability of this life,
faced with the apparent fickleness of fate,
teach me to trust completely in the sure
and certain hope you have given in Christ,
for his name's sake.

Nick Fawcett

May you be blessed by the Lord,
the Maker of heaven and earth

Psalm 115:15

The Lord gives strength to his people;
the Lord blesses his people with peace

Psalm 29:11

Sometimes we have no energy
or health to pray,
but that is when we are upheld
by the love
and prayers of others.

Susan Sayers

Living God,
no matter how helpless
or hopeless I may feel,
teach me that with you by my side,
all things are always less dreadful
than they seem.

Nick Fawcett

The Lord is good,
a stronghold in the day of trouble

Nahum 1:7

Give thanks to the Lord, for he is good.
His love endures for ever

Psalm 136:1

For quiet presence,
for the gift of prayer,
for carer respite,
for words of encouragement
and practical tasks undertaken,
for day trips
and lifetime photo albums shared,
we give thanks for the gift of love
which is the elixir of life.
May we be a friend
to those who need a friend,
modelling our friendship
on your friendship to all.

Siobhán O'Keeffe

Lord Jesus Christ,
as you stilled the storm,
so calm turmoil within me.
Put my mind at rest
and my spirit at peace,
secure in the knowledge
of your never-failing love.

Nick Fawcett

The peace of God, which transcends all understanding
will guard your hearts and minds in Christ Jesus

Philippians 4:7

Surely God is my salvation;
I will trust and not be afraid.
The Lord, the Lord,
is my strength and my song;
he has become my salvation.

Isaiah 12:2

Do not fear, for I have redeemed you;
I have called you by name, you are mine.
When you pass through the waters
I will be with you;
and through the rivers,
they shall not overwhelm you;
when you walk through fire
you shall not be burned,
and the flame shall not consume you.
For I am the Lord your God,
the Holy One of Israel,
your Saviour.

Nick Fawcett
Based on Isaiah 43

The Lord will guide you always

Isaiah 58:11

Lord, I come to you in all my need.
I feel so oppressed as I have had
more than my share of scorn,
more than my share of jeers
from the complacent,
of contempt from the proud.

I feel that many of you people
look at me and laugh;
they deride me for my seeming
lack of understanding;
they say that I do not have a voice.

In their arrogance they pass me by
and do not attempt to engage with me;
in their ignorance they lack the insight to know
that I feel and sense all
that is going on around me.

My lips may have fallen silent
but my heart is more fully alive
than ever before.
I know who cares for my wellbeing
and who scorns
the life in my being.

This toxic attitude could stifle my spirit
but I keep my mind and heart fixed on you.
I trust that one day the scales
may fall from their eyes and hearts
when we may all celebrate our oneness in you.

Siobhán O'Keeffe

KEVIN MAYHEW LTD
Buxhall, Stowmarket, Suffolk, IP14 3BW
E-mail: info@kevinmayhewltd.com
Website: www.kevinmayhew.com

9 8 7 6 5 4 3 2 1 0

ISBN 978 1 84867 454 7
Catalogue No. 1501310

Design and illustrations by Chris Coe

Printed and bound in China